BUTTER

Sugar

Shortbread

Shortbread

30 sweet+savory recipes

by **JANN JOHNSON**

illustrations by **BETH ADAMS**

CHRONICLE BOOKS

SAN FRANCISCO

LIBRARY OF CONGRESS
CATALOGING-IN-PUBLICATION DATA:
JOHNSON, JANN.
SHORTBREAD: THIRTY SWEET AND SAVORY RECIPES/
BY JANN JOHNSON; ILLUSTRATIONS BY BETH ADAMS.
P. CM.
INCLUDES INDEX.
ISBN 0-8118-1359-2 (HC)
1. SHORTBREAD. I. TITLE.
TX772.J637 1997
641.8'654—DC21 97-6174
CIP

PRINTED IN HONG KONG.

DESIGNED BY CAROLE GOODMAN

DISTRIBUTED IN CANADA BY RAINCOAST BOOKS
8680 CAMBIE STREET
VANCOUVER, BRITISH COLUMBIA V6P 6M9

10 9 8 7 6 5 4 3 2 1

CHRONICLE BOOKS
85 SECOND STREET
SAN FRANCISCO, CALIFORNIA 94105

WEB SITE:
www.chronbooks.com

dedicated

to Aunt Pauline McBeth Hewitt.

The creative journey with Chronicle Books is a joy. A warm thank-you to Bill LeBlond, Leslie Jonath, Sarah Putman, Carolyn Miller, Beth Adams, Carole Goodman, Mary Ann Gilderbloom, and the good team behind the scenes.

A heartfelt thank-you to friends and colleagues who tested and contributed: Catherine Bacon, Aretha Cantrell, Elton Cantrell, Kim Cox, Pat Dicker, Pam Farrell, George Henry, Bill Jayme, Katie Longfiled, Lillian Kolarnik, Ed Krayer, Donald McDonald, Joan Meyer, Jay Peterson, Heikki Ratalahti, and Pat Ronzone.

Contents

Introduction

shortbread is a delectable Scottish cookie once served only at Christmas and New Year's Eve (Hogmanay). Shaped in round wooden molds often carved with thistles, it was given notched edges to signify the sun and good fortune, and was symbolic of the winter solstice and the turn of the year. Dense, sandy-textured shortbread is tender-crisp, visually appealing, and a gastronomic delight. The short in the name refers to the rich, short dough with its characteristic high proportion of butter. Surprisingly, for all its flavor, shortbread is the quickest of cookies to prepare.

Traditionally made without eggs or leavening, one of the joys of shortbread is its simplicity and boundless adaptability to flavorings. It can easily be made by hand and is the perfect cookie to make in limited circumstances: a ship's galley, a portable camping oven, a kitchen in an RV or motel, a foreign kitchen, or lack of time. I'm often asked to make cookies on the spur of the moment in an unfamiliar kitchen, and simple and sublime shortbread does the trick. (I've memorized a few recipes.)

Part of the magic of food is to delight the senses, and this cookie is the most versatile I know. Sweet shortbread can be molded, rolled and cut out, scored, stamped, and tinted. The baked cookies may be dipped in chocolate and nuts, iced, or sandwiched with a seductive filling. While less traditional savory shortbread is not quite as malleable as sweet shortbread, it may be baked in imaginative ways, too, and is delicious, dependable, and do-ahead: the ultimate party food.

If this is your first time making shortbread, try the Plain and Simple recipe at an unhurried pace. Enjoy the gift of making something simple. Serve the shortbread on your most beautiful china and invite a friend to tea. When I have very little time before guests arrive, I make one of the simpler shortbread recipes and let it bake while I do something else.

Shortbread keeps so well I carry a nibble when I travel and gift wrap some to give my hosts. It is a great cookie to mail overseas or across the continent to a college student. (See pages 14–16 for gift-wrapping and mailing tips.) Store shortbread in an airtight tin, or wrap well in plastic and freeze.

During the holiday season, I keep the centuries-old Scottish tradition of serving shortbread for Christmas and New Year's to ensure good times, good friends, and, perhaps, good fortune.

ingredients

Because shortbread has so few main ingredients, the butter, sugar, flour, and flavorings must be perfectly fresh and of the finest quality.

Try a tasting of several different butters, side by side, to judge the best—you may be surprised. I have used unsalted butter in these recipes and added salt. To use salted butter, eliminate the salt in the sweet shortbread recipes and reduce the salt by half in the savory recipes. Butter freezes well, but be sure to wrap it well, and let it thaw to the proper temperature before using.

The main sugar used here is granulated cane sugar. Superfine sugar may be substituted, but it is much more expensive and rarely necessary.

Unbleached all-purpose flour is my personal choice (it has one less chemical process), but bleached flour is just fine. Bread flour and cake flour were not tested here.

Brown rice flour (not the white Asian type), found in natural foods stores and some supermarkets, is sometimes included in Scottish shortbread recipes for a bit of crunch. If you can't find it, substitute all-purpose flour, cornstarch, or semolina flour. The end result will be different but good.

equipment

Only the basics are needed to make shortbread: a mixing bowl, a large sturdy wooden spoon or an electric mixer, level measuring cups for dry ingredients, a glass measuring cup for liquids (of which there are few in this cookbook), and measuring spoons.

For baking, I prefer tart pans with removable bottoms. You can find them in mail-order catalogs, such as Sur la Table and Williams-Sonoma, and in cooking supply stores. Some of my favorites are an eight-inch round, a four-by-thirteen-inch rectangle, and an eight-inch square. The lift-out bottoms make removing shortbread from the pan easy. Round cake pans and baking sheets for freeform shortbread are fine for most recipes. I often set the pans on a jelly roll pan to help retrieve them from the oven. I prefer shiny aluminum pans, which reflect heat and produce even baking, not the dark ones, which absorb heat and may overcook the outside of shortbread.

Parchment paper is useful for lining baking sheets, and is given as an option to ungreased pans in many recipes here.

To decorate shortbread, look for wooden or porcelain molds, cookie stamps, tools for imprinting clay (reserve these for cooking only), and anything else you can think of to embellish the dough: a cut-crystal glass, forks, or rubber stamps. Decorative rolling pins will also imprint a design on dough to be cut into squares, rectangles, or triangles.

techniques

baking tips

Shortbread is usually baked in a slow oven. The baking times given here are a guide, since ovens vary. A reliable oven thermometer is helpful.

Generally, shortbread that is baked just until set will be tender. If you prefer a crisper, firmer shortbread (to dunk into coffee or wine like biscotti), bake it 5 to 10 minutes longer than suggested (make notes in this book as a reminder). Increased baking time removes moisture from shortbread and gives it longer keeping qualities as well.

Mix shortbread dough at low speed to avoid incorporating air into the cookie.

If the butter is cold (straight from the refrigerator or freezer), slice it and scatter it on a plate to soften it slightly. The temperature of the room will affect the time it takes. The butter should be softened enough to mix well with other ingredients, but not so soft that it becomes greasy. Room temperature is too soft.

Well-wrapped dough may be frozen for up to three weeks. Let the dough soften for fifteen to twenty minutes at room temperature or in the refrigerator to allow it to be handled (or sliced, if making refrigerator logs) without crumbling.

using molds + special pans

Wooden molds are used to decorate dough before baking. To use a wooden mold, lightly flour it (I use a pastry brush dipped in flour), then press the dough in firmly. Place a baking sheet over the mold and, holding both, turn them over. The dough should unmold; give it a sharp tap if it doesn't. Refrigerate the unmolded dough in the refrigerator for about fifteen minutes to help preserve the design details when baked.

Some porcelain molded pans are designed for use during baking. Follow the manufacturer's instructions. The molds are usually lightly greased and floured first.

Experiment with mini muffin pans for hors d'oeuvres. Pinch off balls of dough and press one into each little well; garnish each with an appropriate tidbit, such as a sliver of herb or nut, if you wish.

decorating tips

To dip cookies in chocolate: Melt 1 tablespoon butter to 4 ounces chopped chocolate in a microwave, or in a double boiler over barely simmering water, stirring until melted. Place the warm chocolate in a coffee mug, Pyrex measuring cup, or another heatproof container and dip each cookie in the chocolate (and in finely chopped nuts, if you wish). Place the cookies on a sheet of waxed paper. Let sit at room temperature, or place in the refrigerator for about 15 minutes to set the chocolate.

To sandwich cookies with fillings (such as chocolate ganache, lemon curd, or jam): Begin by baking small, sturdily shaped cookies. Shortbread crumbles easily, so take care that delicate stems or tips do not break off when handled. Warm fillings spread more easily. Use gentle pressure when sandwiching cookies.

To cut shortbread decoratively: Use a large, sharp, thin knife. To cut a round of shortbread into wedges: Cut the round in half, then cut each half into halves or thirds. Sweet shortbread cuts more easily than savory.

gift ideas

One of my favorite ways to give shortbread is to package it with related items:

Include a baking cookbook with a bottle of premium vanilla extract, or present the shortbread and all the ingredients needed to make it in an old-fashioned mixing bowl.

For the novice baker, fill a gift basket with baking basics to last a lifetime: top-quality measuring cups and spoons, an unusual dish towel, an ornamental pan.

For the advanced baker, give a basket with hard-to-find spices and exotic extracts (my friends give me these from their travels), and fancy cookie cutters, stamps, or molds.

Fill a small, handsome box (lined with waxed

paper to prevent grease marks) with stamped shortbread and tie the box with a large taffeta bow. Wrap a new cookie stamp (a duplicate of the one used) and tie it to the bow.

Use clear plastic boxes to show off a sampler of decorative shortbreads. Tie with an attractive cord or raffia.

Fill a beautiful teapot with shortbread and a fine tea (each packaged in cellophane bags and tied with ribbon in the teapot's colors).

Custom paint a mug and fill with fragrant shortbread cookies.

For quick gifts, fill clear cellophane bags with shortbread and tie with raffia.

tips for mailing shortbread

Shortbread can be mailed whole or cut into serving pieces. (Sweet shortbread is more stable than savory shortbread and ships better. Firm, slightly overbaked shortbread keeps longer and ships better than tender, underbaked short-bread.) Each piece should be wrapped in waxed paper or plastic wrap, then in bubble wrap. Fit the shortbread snugly into a box or tin and seal tightly. Label the box or tin and place it inside a larger box filled with popcorn or recyclable Styrofoam peanuts. Tape the box shut and mark it "perishable."

Sweet Shortbread

traditional shortbread is delicately sweet and buttery rich, and a small, graceful serving is satisfying. (I'm not surprised that something so practical is Scottish!)

Certain sweet shortbreads seem to go with the seasons. I serve Drambuie-Raisin Shortbread on a frosty cold day with a mug of hot, strong coffee. Lavender-Rose Shortbread and Green Tea Shortbread are more delicate and seem better suited for warm weather, with tea in a pretty china cup. Peanut Butter and Molasses Shortbread with Chocolate Glaze is perfect any time of year, dunked in an after-school glass of ice cold milk.

What follows are twenty of my favorite recipes for sweet shortbread. I hope you will take pleasure in making them. A simple act, well done, is deeply satisfying.

plain+simple
SHORTBREAD

Preheat the oven to 300 degrees F. Lightly butter an 8-inch round pan, preferably one with a removable bottom, or use an ungreased or parchment-lined baking sheet. In a medium bowl, with an electric mixer on low speed or a wooden spoon, beat the butter until light in color, about 1 minute. Gradually mix in the sugar, salt, and vanilla. Scrape down the sides of the bowl with a rubber spatula. Gradually mix in the flour until just combined.

Press the dough evenly into the pan, and use the back of a soup spoon to smooth the surface of the dough. Or, pat the dough into an 8-inch round on the baking sheet and decoratively score or flute the edges. Prick the dough attractively with a fork.

Bake in the center of the oven for about 45 minutes, or until just golden around the edges. Place the pan on a wire rack and let the shortbread cool completely. Transfer the shortbread to a cutting board. With a sharp, thin knife, cut into 12 wedges.

makes 12 wedges

SCENTED-SUGAR SHORTBREAD: Delete the vanilla and replace the sugar with a scented sugar.

To make scented sugar, pour a 1-inch layer of granulated sugar into a pint glass jar with a lid, then sprinkle with a flavoring, such as pieces of a split vanilla bean, citrus peels, or scented geranium leaves. Continue to layer sugar and flavoring until the jar is filled. Cap tightly and let sit at room temperature for 1 to 2 weeks.

makes about 2 cups

When the mood hits for a simple bit of sweet, this is good to make. It is an easy introduction to making shortbread (perfect to make with children) and uses ingredients usually on hand.

$1/2$ cup (1 stick)
unsalted butter, softened
$1/3$ cup
sugar
$1/4$ teaspoon
salt
1 teaspoon
vanilla extract
1 cup
all-purpose flour

There are many recipes for Scottish shortbread, but this is the most authentic one I know. It is named to honor my mother's clan.

This dough can be baked in a traditional round and cut into wedges (like the Plain and Simple Shortbread recipe on page 21) or made into cookies using a cookie stamp (I use a thistle design). A sprinkle of large-grained sugar, known as pearl sugar or perlsocker, is the finishing touch.

Preheat the oven to 300 degrees F. In a small bowl, whisk together the rice flour and all-purpose flour to combine; set aside. In a medium bowl, with an electric mixer on low speed or a wooden spoon, beat the butter until light in color, about 1 minute. Mix in the sugar, salt, and vanilla extract. Scrape down the sides of the bowl with a rubber spatula. Gradually mix in the flours until just combined.

Turn the dough out onto a lightly floured board and knead a few times. Pinch into 1-inch pieces, roll them into balls, and place 2 inches apart on an ungreased or parchment-lined baking sheet. Press the balls with a cookie stamp or the bottom of a glass until dough is $^1/_4$ inch thick. Lightly sprinkle each cookie with sugar. Refrigerating the stamped cookies for 10 minutes will help preserve the detail.

Bake in the center of the oven for about 11 to 14 minutes, or until pale golden at the edges. Let the cookies cool on the baking sheet for about 2 minutes, then transfer them to a wire rack to cool completely.

makes about 36 cookies

$^1/_3$ cup
rice flour
$1^1/_3$ cups
all-purpose flour
$^3/_4$ cup ($1^1/_2$ sticks)
unsalted butter, softened
$^1/_2$ cup
granulated sugar
$^1/_4$ teaspoon
salt
$1^1/_2$ teaspoons
vanilla extract
for sprinkling
pearl or granulated sugar

Preheat the oven to 275 degrees F. Lightly butter an 8-inch round pan, preferably one with a removable bottom. In a small bowl, whisk the all-purpose flour and rice flour together; set aside.

In a medium bowl, with an electric mixer on low speed or a wooden spoon, beat the butter until light in color, about 1 minute. Gradually mix in the brown sugar and salt. Add the Scotch or vanilla and continue beating until mixture is well combined. Scrape down the sides of the bowl with a rubber spatula. Gradually mix in the flours until just combined. The dough will be soft.

Press the dough evenly into the pan, and use the back of a soup spoon to smooth the surface of the dough. Holding the pan in one hand and rotating it as if on a lazy susan (or use the real thing), use a dinner fork to score the dough around the outer edge. (Repeat with concentric circles if you wish.)

Bake in the center of the oven for about 55 minutes, or until pale golden. Place the pan on a wire rack and let the shortbread cool completely. Transfer the shortbread from the pan to a cutting board.

With a sharp, thin knife, cut into 16 wedges.

makes 16 wedges

TIP: For a giddy Scotch glaze, mix ⅓ cup sifted confectioners' sugar and 1 tablespoon Scotch to make a glaze. Dribble over the top. After 24 hours, most of the alcohol has evaporated, but the Scotch flavor will remain.

Savor the high proportion of butter, brown sugar flavor, and wee bit of Scotch in this shortbread.

1 cup all-purpose **flour**

2 tablespoons **rice flour**

³/₄ cup (1¹/₂ sticks) **unsalted butter, softened**

¹/₂ cup **packed dark brown sugar**

¹/₄ teaspoon **salt**

1 teaspoon **Scotch or vanilla extract**

lavender-rose
SHORTBREAD

Preheat the oven to 300 degrees F. Lightly butter an 8-inch round pan, preferably one with a removable bottom, or use an ungreased or parchment-lined baking sheet. In a medium bowl, with an electric mixer on low speed or a wooden spoon, beat the butter until light in color, about 1 minute. Mix in the confectioners' sugar, salt, and rose or vanilla extract and continue beating until smooth. Scrape down the sides of the bowl with a rubber spatula. Gradually mix in the flour until just combined.

Press the dough evenly into the pan, use the back of a soup spoon to smooth the surface of the dough. Or, pat the dough into an 8-inch round on the baking sheet and decoratively score or flute the edges. Prick the dough attractively with a fork.

Bake in the center of the oven for about 45 minutes, or until set and firm to a light touch. Place the pan on a wire rack and let the shortbread cool completely. Transfer the shortbread from the pan to a cutting board. With a sharp, thin knife, cut into 16 wedges.

makes 16 wedges

TIPS: Buy organic lavender from a natural foods store or spice market.

Rose extract, not to be confused with rose water, is also known as rose essence and is available in British and Indian shops and by mail. I have also found it in natural foods stores.

The fresh, clean scent of lavender flavors these cookies in a surprisingly delicious way. A touch of rose makes this shortbread unique. Serve with jasmine or flowery assam tea for an afternoon treat.

$^1/_2$ cup (1 stick)
unsalted butter, softened
$^1/_2$ cup
confectioners' sugar
$^1/_8$ teaspoon
salt
$^1/_4$ teaspoon
rose extract OR $^1/_2$ teaspoon vanilla extract
1 cup
all-purpose flour
1 teaspoon
dried organic lavender flowers

drambuie-raisin
SHORTBREAD

In a small bowl, stir the Drambuie or brandy and raisins to mix. Cover and let sit for as long as possible, up to 24 hours. Preheat the oven to 300 degrees F. Lightly butter an 8-inch round pan, preferably one with a removable bottom.

In a medium bowl, with an electric mixer on low speed or a wooden spoon, beat the butter until light in color, about 1 minute. Gradually mix in the sugar and salt. Scrape down the sides of the mixing bowl with a rubber spatula. Gradually mix in the flour until just combined. Stir in the raisins and any remaining Drambuie or brandy.

Press the dough evenly into the pan, and use the back of a soup spoon to smooth the surface of the dough. With a dinner fork, score a mark down the center of the dough and score a parallel mark, evenly spaced, on either side. Give the pan a quarter turn and repeat with 3 marks straight across the first ones to form a "plaid."

Bake in the center of the oven for about 45 minutes, or until pale golden. Place the pan on a wire rack and let the shortbread cool completely. Transfer the shortbread from the pan to a cutting board. With a sharp, thin knife, cut into 16 wedges.

makes 16 wedges

TIP: You can buy liqueurs such as Drambuie in miniature bottles to use just for baking.

Drambuie is an ancient liqueur from the Scottish Isle of Skye made from Scotch, heather honey, and herbs. Raisins steeped in it, preferably overnight, give a tipsy top note to this shortbread. Additional Drambuie, lightly brushed on the cooled cookie, is also scrumptious.

2 tablespoons **Drambuie or brandy**

Heaping 1/3 cup **golden raisins, chopped**

$\frac{1}{2}$ cup (1 stick) + 2 tablespoons **unsalted butter, softened**

6 tablespoons **sugar**

$\frac{1}{4}$ teaspoon **salt**

$1\frac{1}{3}$ cups **all-purpose flour**

oatmeal-pear
SHORTBREAD

Preheat the oven to 300 degrees F. Butter an 8-inch round pan, preferably one with a removable bottom. In a large bowl, with an electric mixer on low speed or a wooden spoon, beat the butter until light in color, about 1 minute. Gradually stir in the brown sugar, vanilla, and salt. Scrape down the sides of the bowl with a rubber spatula. Gradually mix in the oats and flour until just combined. Stir in the chopped pears.

Press the dough evenly into the pan, and use the back of a soup spoon to smooth the surface of the dough. Bake in the center of the oven for about 45 minutes, or until pale golden. Place the pan on a wire rack and let the shortbread cool completely. Transfer the shortbread from the pan to a cutting board. With a sharp, thin knife, cut into 12 wedges.

makes 12 wedges

TIPS: Choose dried fruit that is plump and pliable, preferably organic fruits dried without sulfur.

Dried fruit such as cherries or apricots may be substituted for the dried pears. Muscat raisins are also good.

On a cold, blustery day, this homey shortbread, studded with toothsome bits of dried pear, is ambrosial served warm with a frothy cup of hot chocolate or cider. Try it for breakfast also.

$^1/_2$ cup (1 stick)
unsalted butter, softened
$^1/_2$ cup
packed dark brown sugar
1 teaspoon
vanilla extract
$^1/_4$ teaspoon
salt
1 cup
old-fashioned oats
$^3/_4$ cup
all-purpose flour
$^1/_2$ cup chopped (about 3 pieces)
dried pears

fruit+sunflower seed

Dried apples, pears, apricots, peaches, and prunes are colorful, healthful, and luscious. I add dried cherries, figs, dates, or Muscat raisins to packaged mixed dried fruit. Crunchy dried fruits, such as banana chips, are not suitable for this recipe, however.

The sunflower seeds or nuts sprinkled on top will toast during baking, which enhances their flavor.

Preheat the oven to 300 degrees F. Lightly butter an 8-inch round pan, preferably one with a removable bottom. In a medium bowl, with an electric mixer on low speed or a wooden spoon, beat the butter until creamy, about 1 minute. Mix in the sugar, salt, and liqueur or extract and continue beating until the mixture is smooth. Scrape down the sides of the bowl with a rubber spatula. Gradually mix in the flour until just combined. Stir in the dried fruit. The dough will be sticky.

Press the dough evenly into the pan, and use the back of a soup spoon to smooth the surface of the dough. Sprinkle the sunflower seeds or macadamia nuts over the top and press in lightly.

Bake in the center of the oven for about 45 minutes, or until golden. Place the pan on a wire rack and let the shortbread cool completely. Transfer the shortbread from the pan to a cutting board. With a sharp, thin knife, cut into 16 wedges.

makes 16 wedges

TIPS: Look for plump organic fruit dried without sulfur.

Pear de Pear liqueur is a pear brandy with a natural affinity for fruit desserts. Pear eau-de-vie and Poire Williams can also be used.

$^1/_2$ cup (1 stick)
  unsalted butter, softened
$^1/_3$ cup
  packed light brown sugar
$^1/_4$ teaspoon
  salt
1 teaspoon
  Pear de Pear liqueur or vanilla extract
1 cup
  all-purpose flour
$^1/_2$ cup
  mixed dried fruit, coarsely chopped
$^1/_4$ cup
  hulled sunflower seeds or chopped macadamia nuts

cranberry
SHORTBREAD

Preheat the oven to 275 degrees F. Lightly butter an 8-inch round pan, preferably one with a removable bottom. In a food processor, pulse the sugar, salt, and cranberries until finely chopped. Add the butter and pulse until incorporated. Scrape down the sides of the bowl with a rubber spatula. Gradually mix in the flour until just combined. Or, to make by hand, mince the cranberries with a sharp knife and mix with the sugar. In a medium bowl, with an electric mixer on low speed or a wooden spoon, beat the butter until creamy, about 1 minute. Blend in the cranberry mixture. Stir in the salt and flour.

Press the dough evenly into the pan, and use the back of a soup spoon to smooth the surface of the dough. Sprinkle with the sugar.

Bake in the center of the oven for about 50 minutes, or until firm to a light touch but not browned. Place the pan on a wire rack and let the shortbread cool completely. Transfer the shortbread from the pan to a cutting board. With a sharp, thin knife, cut into 16 wedges.

makes 16 wedges

TIP: Dried cranberries may be used, but the shortbread will not be pink.

Cranberries tint this shortbread a radiant, soft pink and make it a good choice to serve on warm autumn afternoons and during the winter holidays with a piping hot cup of tea.

$^1/_2$ cup
sugar
$^1/_8$ teaspoon
salt
$^1/_2$ cup
fresh cranberries
$^1/_2$ cup (1 stick)
unsalted butter, softened
1 cup
all-purpose flour
for sprinkling
pearl sugar or granulated sugar

r u m - l i m e
SHORTBREAD

Preheat the oven to 300 degrees F. Lightly butter an 8-inch round pan, preferably one with a removable bottom, or use an ungreased or parchment-lined baking sheet. In a medium bowl, with an electric mixer on low speed or a wooden spoon, beat the butter until creamy, about 1 minute. Mix in the brown sugar, salt, and zest. Scrape down the sides of the bowl with a rubber spatula. Gradually mix in the flour until just combined.

Press the dough evenly into the pan, and use the back of a soup spoon to smooth the surface of the dough. Or, pat the dough into an 8-inch round on the baking sheet and score or flute the edges. Decoratively mark and prick the dough with a fork.

Bake in the center of the oven for about 45 minutes, or until set and firm to a light touch. Place the pan on a wire rack and brush the shortbread with the rum glaze. Let cool completely. Transfer the shortbread from the pan to a cutting board. With a sharp, thin knife, cut into 16 wedges.

makes 16 wedges

RUM GLAZE: Mix 2 teaspoons dark rum or 1 teaspoon rum extract and 1 teaspoon water with $^1/_3$ cup sifted confectioners' sugar until smooth. Add drops of water or lime juice, if needed, to adjust the consistency similar to light cream. Cover until use.

makes about $^1/_4$ cup

TIP: You can substitute fresh lime juice for the rum. The shortbread is also delicious without the glaze.

On the hottest days of the year, offer refreshing iced tea and Rum-Lime Shortbread and hope for a balmy breeze. Limes seem quintessentially tropical to me, perhaps because they were plentiful in the Caribbean and South Pacific, where I lived as a child.

$^1/_2$ cup (1 stick) **unsalted butter, softened**
$^1/_2$ cup **packed light brown sugar**
$^1/_4$ teaspoon **salt**
1 tablespoon **lime zest, finely grated**
$1^1/_4$ cups **all-purpose flour**

Rum Glaze (recipe follows)

mexican chocolate

SHORTBREAD

Preheat the oven to 300 degrees F. Lightly butter an 8-inch round pan, preferably one with a removable bottom, or use an ungreased or parchment-lined baking sheet. In a medium bowl, with an electric mixer on low speed or a wooden spoon, beat the butter until light in color, about 1 minute. Mix in the brown sugar, cocoa, cinnamon, salt, and almond and vanilla extracts, and continue beating until the mixture is smooth. Scrape down the sides of the bowl with a rubber spatula. Gradually mix in the almonds and flour until just combined.

Press the dough evenly into the pan, and use the back of a soup spoon to smooth the surface of the dough. Or, pat the dough into an 8-inch round on the baking sheet and decoratively score or flute the edges. Prick the dough attractively with a fork.

Bake in the center of the oven for about 45 minutes, or until set and firm to a light touch. Place the pan on a wire rack and let the shortbread cool completely. Transfer the shortbread from the pan to a cutting board. With a sharp, thin knife, cut into 12 wedges.

makes 12 wedges

NUTLESS MEXICAN CHOCOLATE SHORTBREAD: For a cookie without nuts, omit the almonds and add ¹/₄ cup more all-purpose flour.

In Central and South America, where chocolate originated, hot chocolate is often flavored with cinnamon, vanilla, and almonds and sweetened with *piloncillo,* **or unrefined Mexican sugar. In this shortbread, brown sugar adds a similar taste.**

¹/₂ cup (1 stick) + 2 tablespoons **unsalted butter, softened**

¹/₂ cup **packed light brown sugar**

3 tablespoons **unsweetened cocoa powder**

¹/₄ teaspoon **ground cinnamon**

¹/₄ teaspoon **salt**

¹/₄ teaspoon **almond extract**

¹/₄ teaspoon **vanilla extract**

¹/₄ cup finely chopped **almonds**

1 cup **all-purpose flour**

green tea
SHORTBREAD

Preheat the oven to 275 degrees F. Line a baking sheet with parchment paper. In a small bowl, whisk together the all-purpose flour and rice flour; set aside. In a medium bowl, with an electric mixer on low speed or a wooden spoon, beat the butter until light in color, about 1 minute. Gradually mix in the confectioners' sugar and salt. Add the vanilla extract and continue beating until the mixture is smooth and creamy. Add the green tea powder and the optional green food coloring. Scrape down the sides of the bowl with a rubber spatula. Gradually mix in the flours until just combined.

Turn the dough out onto a lightly floured board and knead in any loose crumbs. Pinch the dough into $1\frac{1}{2}$-inch pieces and roll them into balls. Place them 1 inch apart on the baking sheet. Press the cookies with a cookie stamp or the bottom of a glass (especially one with a decorative bottom).

Bake in the center of the oven for about 13 to 15 minutes, or until set but not colored. Let the cookies cool on the baking sheet for about 2 minutes, then transfer them to a wire rack to cool completely.

makes about 18 cookies

TIP: Look for exquisite chrysanthemum molds, sold in Japanese shops, to shape the dough, or roll the dough $\frac{1}{4}$ inch thick and use small flower-shaped cookie cutters such as those used for making gum paste flowers.

Green tea, which is unfermented black tea, is available in powder form in Japanese markets. It gives a delicate flavor and a celadon color to this shortbread. Serve green tea shortbread with exotic sorbets and ice creams such as mango, guava, and passion fruit.

1 cup
all-purpose flour
$\frac{1}{4}$ cup
rice flour
$\frac{1}{2}$ cup (1 stick) +
1 tablespoon
unsalted butter, softened
$\frac{1}{2}$ cup
confectioners' sugar
$\frac{1}{4}$ teaspoon
salt
1 teaspoon
vanilla extract
$1\frac{1}{2}$ tablespoons
green tea powder
2 drops
green food coloring (optional)

meyer lemon—macadamia

Preheat the oven to 300 degrees F. Lightly butter a 9-inch square pan, or use an ungreased or parchment-lined baking sheet. In a large bowl, with an electric mixer on low speed or a wooden spoon, beat the butter until light in color, about 1 minute. Mix in the sugar, salt, lemon and vanilla extracts, and zest and continue beating until the mixture is smooth. Scrape down the sides of the bowl with a rubber spatula. Gradually mix in the flour until just combined.

Press the dough evenly into the pan, and use the back of a soup spoon to smooth the surface of the dough. Or, pat the dough into a 9-inch square on the baking sheet and decoratively score or flute the edges. Sprinkle with the macadamia nuts and press lightly.

Bake in the center of the oven for about 45 minutes, until set and pale golden. Place the pan on a wire rack and let the shortbread cool completely. Transfer the shortbread from the pan to a cutting board. With a sharp, thin knife, cut into 16 squares.

makes 16 squares

TIP: The more familiar Lisbon or Eureka lemon can be used, but the flavor will be sharper.

The lemon of choice for many chefs, the Meyer lemon is round and golden yellow, with a thin skin. Its sweet taste pairs well with Australia's remarkable botanical gift, buttery, crunchy macadamia nuts.

1 cup (2 sticks) **unsalted butter, softened**

²/₃ cup **sugar**

¹/₂ teaspoon **salt**

¹/₂ teaspoon **lemon extract**

¹/₂ teaspoon **vanilla extract**

1 tablespoon **meyer lemon zest, finely grated**

2 cups **all-purpose flour**

¹/₂ cup **chopped macadamia nuts**

Preheat the oven to 325 degrees F. Line an 8-inch round pan with a piece of plastic wrap, letting the excess hang over the sides. In a medium bowl, with an electric mixer on low speed or a wooden spoon, beat the butter until light in color, about 1 minute. Mix in the brown sugar, salt, and vanilla extract. Scrape down the sides of the bowl with a rubber spatula. Gradually mix in the flour until just combined.

Press half of the dough evenly into the pre-pared pan, and use the back of a soup spoon to smooth the surface of the dough. Refrigerate for 10 minutes. Pull up on the plastic wrap to lift the dough out of the pan and onto a baking sheet (discard the plastic wrap). Lightly butter the pan and press the remaining half of the dough evenly into the bottom of the pan. Again, use the back of a soup spoon to smooth the surface of the dough.

In a small bowl, stir the peanut butter and molasses together until smooth. Evenly spread the peanut butter mixture over the dough in the pan to within $1/2$ inch of the edge. Place the remaining round of dough into the pan on top of the peanut butter filling. Press down the edges with a fork to seal.

Bake in the center of the oven for about 30 minutes, or until golden. Place the pan on a wire rack and let the shortbread cool completely. Transfer the shortbread from the pan to a cutting board. Drizzle warm chocolate glaze over the top. Let the chocolate set, then cut the shortbread into 12 wedges with a sharp, thin knife.

makes 12 wedges

A rich filling of peanut butter and molasses is the sweet surprise in this short-bread. Drizzle choco-late glaze over the cookie for a decadent delight.

$1/2$ cup (1 stick)
  unsalted butter, softened
$1/2$ cup
  packed dark brown sugar
$1/4$ teaspoon
  salt
2 teaspoons
  vanilla extract
$1 1/4$ cups
  all-purpose flour
$1/4$ cup
  creamy peanut butter
2 tablespoons
  molasses

Chocolate Glaze
(recipe follows)

CHOCOLATE GLAZE: In a small saucepan over medium heat, bring ¼ cup heavy cream to a boil and remove from heat. Chop 3 ounces bittersweet chocolate and add to the cream. Cover and let set for 10 minutes. Stir to blend well. Keep warm over warm water if necessary.

makes about ½ cup

TIP: To ice the sides of the shortbread as well, cut the shortbread into wedges and slightly separate them before drizzling with the glaze.

white chocolate+black raspberry

Preheat the oven to 300 degrees F. Butter, then line an 8-inch round pan with plastic wrap, letting the excess hang over the edge. In a medium bowl, with an electric mixer on low speed or a wooden spoon, beat the butter until light in color, about 1 minute. Mix in the confectioners' sugar, salt, and vanilla extract. Scrape down the sides of the bowl with a rubber spatula. Gradually mix in the flour until just combined.

Firmly press half the dough evenly into the lined pan, and use the back of a soup spoon to smooth the surface of the dough. Refrigerate 10 minutes. Then, grasping the plastic wrap, lift up the round of dough out onto the baking sheet (discard the plastic wrap). Press the remaining half of the dough evenly into the pan. Again, use the back of a soup spoon to smooth the surface of the dough.

Evenly spread raspberry jam over the dough in pan to within $^1/_2$ inch of the edge. Sprinkle the jam evenly with the chopped white chocolate. Place the remaining round of dough into the pan on top of the filling. Let the dough stand a few minutes to soften, then press the edges with a fork to seal.

Bake in the center of the oven for about 45 minutes, or until set but not colored. Place the pan on a wire rack and let the shortbread cool completely. Transfer the shortbread from the pan to a cutting board. With a sharp, thin knife, cut into 16 wedges.

makes 16 wedges

When this opulent shortbread is sliced, a beautiful filling of white chocolate and raspberry is revealed. Bittersweet chocolate may be substitued for the white chocolate.

$^1/_2$ cup (1 stick) + 2 tablespoons
   unsalted butter, softened
$^1/_4$ cup
   confectioners' sugar
$^1/_4$ teaspoon
   salt
1 teaspoon
   vanilla extract
$1^1/_3$ cups
   all-purpose flour
$^1/_3$ cup
   black raspberry jam
3 ounces
   white chocolate, finely chopped

java-honey

SHORTBREAD

Coffee-scented shortbread dough makes great refrigerator cookies, and each slice can be pressed with a bee or beehive cookie stamp. Honey, like sugar, can be caramelized, and dries to a beautiful high gloss.

In a medium bowl, dissolve the instant coffee in the hot water. In a medium bowl, with an electric mixer on low speed or a wooden spoon, add the butter and beat until light in color, about 1 minute. Mix in the brown sugar, salt, and cinnamon and continue beating until the mixture is smooth. Scrape down the sides of the bowl with a rubber spatula. Gradually mix in the flour until just combined.

Divide the dough in half and roll each portion into a 5-inch-long log. Cover with waxed paper or plastic wrap and refrigerate until firm, at least 2 hours or overnight.

Preheat the oven to 300 degrees F. Slice the dough 1/4 inch thick and place the cookies 1 inch apart on an ungreased or parchment-lined baking sheet. Press with a cookie stamp.

Bake in the center of the oven for about 12 to 15 minutes, or until firm to a light touch. Let the cookies cool for about 2 minutes on the baking sheet, then transfer them from the pan to a wire rack to cool completely.

In a small saucepan, heat the honey to boiling and cook *just* until honey begins to darken (if it's too dark, it will be bitter). Immediately remove from heat. Be careful; the honey will be very hot. Let the honey cool a bit and brush the warm honey over each cookie. It will dry to a shiny, slightly tacky finish. (High hunidity will cause stickiness.) The cookies should not be stacked.

makes about 40 cookies

TIP: This shortbread also looks beautiful rolled 1/4 inch thick, cut out with hexagonal cutters, and stamped.

1 tablespoon
instant coffee granules

1 teaspoon
hot water

1/2 cup (1 stick)
unsalted butter, softened

1/3 cup
light brown sugar

1/4 teaspoon
salt

pinch
ground cinnamon

1 cup
all-purpose flour

1/4 cup
honey

chocolate-coconut

Preheat the oven to 300 degrees F. Lightly butter an 8-inch round pan, preferably one with a removable bottom. In a medium bowl, with an electric mixer on low speed or a wooden spoon, beat the butter until light in color, about 1 minute. Mix in the brown sugar, salt, cocoa powder and vanilla extract. Scrape down the sides of the bowl with a rubber spatula. Gradually mix in the flour until just combined.

Press dough evenly into the pan, and use the back of a soup spoon to smooth the surface of the dough.

To make the topping: In a small bowl, with an electric mixer on low speed or a wooden spoon, beat the confectioners' sugar, egg white, and vanilla together. Spread the topping evenly over the surface of the shortbread. Sprinkle evenly with the coconut.

Bake in the center of the oven for about 45 minutes, or until set and firm to a light touch. Place the pan on a wire rack and let the shortbread cool completely. Transfer the shortbread from the pan to a cutting board. With a sharp, thin knife, cut into 16 wedges.

makes 16 wedges

This delectable deep-brown chocolate shortbread has a baked-on ivory-colored coconut topping. Serve it with a cappuccino or cafè latte.

$^1/_2$ cup (1 stick) + 1 tablespoon **unsalted butter, softened**

$^1/_3$ cup **packed light brown sugar**

$^1/_4$ teaspoon **salt**

3 tablespoons **unsweetened cocoa powder**

1$^1/_2$ teaspoons **vanilla extract**

1 cup **all-purpose flour**

COCONUT TOPPING

$^1/_2$ cup sifted **confectioners' sugar**

1 tablespoon **egg white**

1 teaspoon **vanilla extract**

$^1/_2$ cup **shredded coconut, fresh or packaged**

maple-glazed spice

Preheat the oven to 300 degrees F. Lightly butter an 8-inch round pan, preferably one with a removable bottom, or use an ungreased or parchment-lined baking sheet. In a medium bowl, with an electric mixer on low speed or a wooden spoon, beat the butter until light in color, about 1 minute. Mix in the sugar, ginger, cinnamon, cloves, nutmeg, cardamom, and salt. Scrape down the sides of the bowl with a rubber spatula. Gradually mix in the flour until just combined.

Press the dough evenly into the pan, and use the back of a soup spoon to smooth the surface of the dough. Or, pat the dough into an 8-inch round on the baking sheet and decoratively score or flute the edges. Prick the dough attractively with a fork.

Bake in the center of the oven for about 45 minutes, until set and firm to a light touch. Using a pastry brush, evenly coat the warm shortbread with the glaze. Place the pan on a wire rack and let the shortbread cool completely. Transfer the shortbread from the pan to a cutting board. With a sharp, thin knife, cut into 16 wedges.

makes 16 wedges

MAPLE GLAZE: In a small bowl, whisk 2 tablespoons maple syrup and 3 tablespoons sifted confectioners' sugar together until mixed. Cover until use.

makes 3 tablespoons

This spicy shortbread, with its thin polish of translucent maple icing, is good served with hot apple cider.

$^1/_2$ cup (1 stick) **unsalted butter, softened**

$^1/_2$ cup **light brown sugar**

$^1/_2$ teaspoon **ground ginger**

$^1/_2$ teaspoon **cinnamon**

$^1/_4$ teaspoon **ground cloves**

$^1/_4$ teaspoon **nutmeg**

$^1/_8$ teaspoon **ground cardamom**

$^1/_8$ teaspoon **salt**

1 cup **all-purpose flour**

Maple Glaze (recipe follows)

CHINESE FIVE-SPICE SHORTBREAD: Serve this shortbread, with its spicy anise flavor, with a smoky Chinese tea. Substitute ³/₄ teaspoon Chinese Five-Spice powder for the ginger, cinnamon, cloves, nutmeg, and cardamom. Chinese Five-Spice powder is available in the ethnic foods section of many supermarkets, or in Asian food stores. This shortbread is best unglazed.

CHOCOLATE
DIPPED

Preheat the oven to 300 degrees F. Lightly butter a 4-by-13-inch tart pan, preferably one with a removable bottom, or line a baking sheet with parchment paper. In a large bowl, with an electric mixer on low speed or a wooden spoon, beat the butter until light in color, about 1 minute. Gradually mix in the sugar, salt, and zest. Add the orange extract and continue beating until the mixture is creamy. Scrape down the sides of the bowl with a rubber spatula. Gradually mix in the flour until just combined.

Press the dough evenly into the pan, and use the back of a soup spoon to smooth the surface of the dough. Or, pat it into a 4-by-13-inch rectangle on the prepared baking sheet and decoratively score or flute the edges. Use a dinner fork to score the dough lengthwise, covering the entire surface.

Bake in the center of the oven for about 45 minutes, or until pale golden. Place the pan on a wire rack and let cool completely. Transfer the shortbread from the pan to a cutting board. With a sharp, thin knife, cut the rectangle lengthwise down the middle, then cut into 1-inch bars. Dip each bar halfway into the warm chocolate and set on waxed paper to harden.

makes about 26 bars

CHOCOLATE COATING: Place 4 ounces chopped dark chocolate and 1 tablespoon solid vegetable shortening or butter in a microwave-proof cup, microwave on medium for 1 minute, and stir. Microwave on medium, in 20-second intervals, until the chocolate is melted and runny. Or, melt the chocolate and shortening or butter in a

Tangy, tiny clementines are part of the mandarin orange and tangerine family. A generous amount of zest tints this dough a beautiful pale orange and, dipped in chocolate, creates a seductive flavor. These make a sumptuous gift.

$^3/_4$ cup
($1^1/_2$ sticks)
**unsalted butter,
softened**

$^2/_3$ cup
sugar

$^1/_4$ teaspoon
salt

$^1/_4$ cup minced
clementine zest

1 teaspoon
orange extract

$1^1/_2$ cups
all-purpose flour

Chocolate Coating
(recipe follows)

double boiler over barely simmering water.

makes a scant ½ cup

TIPS: Clementine rinds are loosely attached and difficult to grate. Instead, carefully cut off strips of the zest with a sharp vegetable peeler (avoiding the white pith), coarsely chop it, and pulse it in a food processor with the sugar. Or, mince the strips of zest with a sharp knife. Substitute 2 tablespoons grated orange zest for the clementine zest if necessary.

Solid vegetable shortening will give the chocolate coating a slightly higher gloss, but butter will taste better.

almond

These luscious, tender bars are rich with almond paste. The golden burnt sugar icing, with its offbeat, slightly sweet flavor, adds a counterpoint.

Preheat the oven to 300 degrees F. Lightly butter a 4-by-13-inch rectangular pan, preferably one with a removable bottom, or line a baking sheet with parchment paper. In a medium bowl, with an electric mixer on low speed or a wooden spoon, beat the butter until light in color, about 1 minute. Mix in the almond paste and beat until the mixture is smooth. Add the sugar, salt, almond extract, and optional brandy and mix thoroughly. Scrape down the sides of the bowl with a rubber spatula. Gradually mix in the flour until just combined.

Press the dough evenly into the pan, and use the back of a soup spoon to smooth the surface of the dough. Or, pat the dough into a 4-by-13-inch rectangle on the prepared baking sheet and decoratively score or flute the edges. Scatter the almonds over the top of the dough. Press in lightly.

Bake in the center of the oven for about 45 minutes, or until pale golden. Place the pan on a wire rack and let the shortbread cool completely. Transfer the shortbread from the pan to a cutting board. With a sharp, thin knife, cut down the center lengthwise, and then across into 1-inch bars. Drizzle with burnt sugar icing.

makes about 26 bars

BURNT SUGAR ICING: In a small skillet over medium heat, cook 2 tablespoons granulated sugar and 1 tablespoon water until the mixture melts and turns nut brown. (This will happen quickly, so don't leave the pan unattended.) It may bubble up and will be very hot, so take care. Add 1 teaspoon butter and 1 tablespoon

$^3/_4$ cup (1$^1/_2$ sticks)
unsalted butter, softened

$^1/_2$ cup
almond paste, at room temperature

$^1/_3$ cup
sugar

$^1/_4$ teaspoon
salt

$^1/_2$ teaspoon
almond extract

1 teaspoon
brandy (optional)

1$^1/_2$ cups
all-purpose flour

$^1/_3$ cup
sliced almonds

Burnt Sugar Icing (recipe follows)

confectioners' sugar and stir to mix. If necessary, add a bit more water so the icing can be
drizzled.

makes about 3 tablespoons

TIP: A nonstick skillet is useful for caramatiz-
ing sugar, but most have dark surfaces, making
it hard to judge the color of the sugar as it
caramelizes. Have a light-colored saucer near
the skillet to test a drop.

date-hazelnut
SHORTBREAD

Preheat the oven to 325 degrees F. With a sharp knife, halve each date crosswise and stuff each half with a hazelnut; set aside. In a medium bowl, with an electric mixer on low speed or a wooden spoon, beat the butter until light in color, about 1 minute. Gradually beat in the confectioners' sugar, then add the cinnamon and salt and continue beating until the mixture is smooth and creamy. Scrape down the sides of the bowl with a rubber spatula. Gradually mix in the flour until just combined. If necessary, add a few drops of water if the dough seems very stiff.

Turn the dough out onto a lightly floured board and knead a few times to help make it pliable. Pinch the dough off into 24 one-inch pieces. Wrap each stuffed date with a piece of dough, covering it completely and pinching the edges together to seal. Place the cookies 1 inch apart on an ungreased or parchment-lined baking sheet, pinched-side down.

Bake in the center of the oven for about 11 to 14 minutes, or until the cookies are pale golden. Let the cookies cool on the baking sheet for a few minutes, then transfer them to a wire rack to cool completely. Dust with confectioners' sugar.

makes about 24 cookies

TIPS: Giant date palm trees, native to the Middle East, produce several varieties of this sugary fruit. My favorite is the Medjool I find in California farmer's markets (they are large, so cut them into thirds for this recipe). Look for

Sweet, plump dates are stuffed with hazelnuts, then wrapped in a cinnamon-scented dough. Whole almonds, cut in half, or macadamia nuts are also a good choice.

12 **pitted dates, skinned**
24 **hazelnuts, skinned**
$1/2$ cup (1 stick) +
2 tablespoons
   **unsalted butter,
   softened**
$1/4$ cup
   **confectioners'
   sugar, + extra
   to dust cookies**
$1/4$ teaspoon
   ground cinnamon
$1/4$ teaspoon
   salt
$1 1/4$ cups
   all-purpose flour

dates that haven't hardened or formed sugar crystals.

To remove the bitter brown skin of the hazelnuts: Bake them in a 350 degrees F oven for about 10 to 15 minutes, transfer them to a clean dish towel (linen is excellent), and rub them until the skins flake off.

Savory Shortbread

savory shortbread is not as traditional as sweet shortbread, but it is so flavorful and easy to make that it has become a tradition with me.

Eye-catching, bite-sized, shortbread appetizers can complement before-dinner drinks and the meal that follows. Try cutting some shortbread into over-sized crackers to serve with soup, or cut shortbread into small cubes to use as croutons in a crisp salad. Slice peppery shortbread into short, fat straws to add bite to a buffet.

To ensure that a platter of savory shortbread doesn't get mistaken for sweet cookies, garnish it with a bulb of garlic, a bright chili pepper, or a sprig of parsley.

In a medium-sized heavy skillet, melt 1 tablespoon of the butter over medium-high heat. When the butter foams, stir in the shallot and sugar and reduce heat to low. Sauté the shallot until dark golden and caramelized, stirring occasionally, about 15 minutes. Remove from heat and sprinkle the vinegar over the shallots. Let cool.

Preheat the oven to 325 degrees F. Lightly butter an 8-inch round pan, preferably one with a removable bottom. In a medium bowl, with an electric mixer on low speed or a wooden spoon, beat the remaining butter and the cheese together until blended. Add the caramelized shallot mixture. Gradually mix in the flour until just combined.

Press the dough evenly into the pan, and use the back of a soup spoon to smooth the surface of the dough. Bake in the center of the oven for about 40 minutes, or until browned lightly. Place the pan on a wire rack and let the shortbread cool completely. Transfer the shortbread from the pan to a cutting board. With a sharp, thin knife, cut into 12 wedges.

makes 12 wedges

Caramelized shallots are irresistibly good in this superb shortbread, while vinegar adds a gentle punch.

$^{1}/_{2}$ cup (1 stick)
unsalted butter, softened
$^{1}/_{3}$ cup
(about 2 ounces)
coarsely chopped shallot
$^{1}/_{2}$ teaspoon
sugar
$^{1}/_{2}$ teaspoon
balsamic or wine vinegar
$^{1}/_{2}$ cup
(about 2 ounces)
shredded Monterey Jack cheese
1 cup
all-purpose flour

corn + pumpkin seed

Preheat the oven to 350 degrees F. Lightly butter an 8-inch round pan, preferably one with a removable bottom. In a medium bowl with an electric mixer on low speed or a wooden spoon, beat the butter until light in color, about 1 minute. Add the cheese, cornmeal, salt, and chile and beat until well combined. Scrape down the sides of the bowl with a rubber spatula. Gradually mix in the flour until just combined.

Press the dough evenly into the pan, and use the back of a soup spoon to smooth the surface of the dough. Sprinkle the pumpkin seeds evenly over the surface and press in firmly. Bake in the center of the oven for about 35 minutes, or until lightly browned around edges. Place the pan on a wire rack and let the shortbread cool completely. Transfer the shortbread from the pan to a cutting board. With a sharp, thin knife, cut into 8 wedges.

makes 8 wedges

TIPS: Ground New Mexico chile can be found in the Mexican section of many food markets.

This shortbread crumbles easily, so it is best to serve it in large portions.

Both pumpkins and corn are native to North America. Golden-green pumpkin seeds, known as pepitas in Mexico, add a crunchy topping to this short-bread. Serve with Mexican soups or grilled meats.

7 tablespoons
unsalted butter, softened

1 cup (about 4 ounces)
shredded Monterey Jack cheese

1/4 cup
yellow or white cornmeal

1/2 teaspoon
salt

1/4 teaspoon
ground new Mexico Chile OR 1/8 teaspoon cayenne pepper

1 cup
all-purpose flour

1/2 cup
salted roasted pumpkin seeds

herbed

In a medium bowl with an electric mixer on medium speed or a wooden spoon, beat the butter until light in color, about 1 minute. Blend in the cheese and salt. Gradually mix in the flour until just combined. Stir in the herbs.

On a sheet of waxed paper, knead the dough a few times. Divide the dough in half. Roll each piece into a 5-inch-long log. Wrap the logs in waxed paper and twist the ends closed. Refrigerate until firm, at least 1 hour or overnight.

Preheat the oven to 350 degrees F. Unwrap the shortbread logs and cut into ¼-inch-thick rounds. Place the rounds 1 inch apart on an ungreased or parchment-lined baking sheet.

Bake in the center of the oven for about 10 to 15 minutes, or until lightly browned. Let the slices cool on the baking sheet for about 2 minutes, then carefully transfer them from the pan to a wire rack.

makes about 40 slices

TIPS: To strip fresh herbs, such as rosemary, of their tiny leaves, hold the top of a sprig with one hand and with the other hand firmly pinch and pull down the stem.

Dried herbs may also be used in this recipe, but cut the amount in half.

Choose a trio of fresh herbs from your garden (or grocer) or a single pungent herb, such as rosemary, to make these green-flecked crackers. They are good alone or as beds for canapés. (Try chive crackers with crème fraîche and caviar or smoked salmon.)

½ cup (1 stick)
  unsalted butter, softened
rounded ½ cup
(about 2 ounces)
  shredded Monterey Jack cheese
½ teaspoon
  salt
1¼ cups
  all-purpose flour
1 tablespoon
  minced fresh herbs

Melt the butter in a small saucepan over medium heat or in a glass measuring cup in a microwave. Remove from heat and stir in the chocolate until melted. Let cool to room temperature.

In a medium bowl, whisk together the flour, cayenne, salt, cinnamon, and garlic. Pour the chocolate mixture over the flour mixture and stir with a wooden spoon until well combined. Refrigerate for a few minutes, if needed, to make a stiffer dough.

On a sheet of waxed paper, roll the dough into a 7-inch-long log. Wrap the dough in waxed paper, twist the ends closed, and refrigerate until firm, at least 1 hour or overnight.

Preheat the oven to 350 degrees F. Unwrap the dough and cut into $1/4$-inch-thick rounds. Place 1 inch apart on an ungreased or parchment-lined baking sheet and bake until crisp, about 13 minutes. Let the slices cool on the baking sheet for about 2 minutes, then carefully transfer them to a wire rack to cool completely.

makes about 28 crackers

TIP: If you prefer mild heat, reduce the cayenne pepper to $1/4$ teaspoon. If you want more punch, increase the cayenne to 1 teaspoon or lightly sprinkle red pepper flakes over the crackers.

Use these smoky medium-hot crackers for canapés, topped with a bit of turkey and pepper jelly, and garnished, perhaps, with a sliver of avocado.

4 tablespoons ($1/2$ stick)
  unsalted butter
1 square
  unsweetened
  finely chopped
  chocolate
$2/3$ cup
  all-purpose flour
$1/2$ teaspoon
  cayenne pepper
$1/4$ teaspoon
  salt
pinch
  ground cinnamon
pinch
  garlic powder

madras curry—coconut

In a medium bowl, with an electric mixer on low speed or a wooden spoon, beat the butter and cream cheese until light in color, about 1 minute. Add the curry powder, salt, and coconut. Gradually mix in the flour until just combined.

On a sheet of waxed paper, knead the dough a few times. Roll the dough into a 9-inch-long log. Wrap in waxed paper and twist the ends closed. Refrigerate until firm, at least 1 hour or overnight.

Preheat the oven to 350 degrees F. Unwrap the shortbread log and cut it into $1/4$-inch-thick slices. Place the slices 1 inch apart on an ungreased or parchment-lined baking sheet. Bake in the center of the oven for about 12 to 15 minutes or until golden. Let the thins cool on the baking sheet for about 2 minutes, then carefully transfer them to a wire rack to cool completely.

makes about 36 thins

TIPS: Madras curry powder is available at some supermarkets and Indian markets.

To add a stronger flavor of curry, sprinkle additional curry powder on the log of dough to lightly coat it before wrapping it in waxed paper.

Madras curry powder is the genuine article, straight from India. Different in flavor, with its hint of anise, from American curry powder, it's a good spice to add to your collection.

Use sweetened coconut here for a sweet-salty contrast. Serve these with a dab of cream cheese and mango-ginger chutney for a choice hors d'oeuvre.

$1/2$ cup (1 stick)
unsalted butter, softened

2 ounces
cream cheese

1 teaspoon
Madras curry powder

$1/4$ teaspoon
salt

$1/3$ cup
finely chopped sweetened shredded coconut

1 cup
all-purpose flour

pecorino
SHORTBREAD

Preheat the oven to 325 degrees F. Lightly butter an 8-inch round pan, preferably one with a removable bottom. In a medium bowl, with an electric mixer on low speed or a wooden spoon, beat the butter until light in color, about 1 minute. Stir in the cheese. Gradually mix in the flour until just combined.

Press the dough evenly into the pan, and use the back of a soup spoon to smooth the surface of the dough. If desired, score the entire surface with a dinner fork. Generously sprinkle the paprika evenly over the top of the dough all the way to the edge.

Bake in the center of the oven for about 35 minutes, or until set and firm to a light touch. Place the pan on a wire rack and let the shortbread cool completely. Transfer the shortbread from the pan to a cutting board. With a sharp, thin knife, cut into 16 wedges.

makes 16 wedges

TIPS: For a milder cheese flavor, use 1/2 cup grated cheese. Softer cheeses work well, too.

For super-flavorful croutons, double the recipe and bake in a 8-inch square pan. Cut into $1/2$-inch squares.

Pecorino, with its top note of lemon, is used generously for these shortbread crisps, but you can substitute other grating cheeses, such as Parmigiano-Reggiano or dry Monterey Jack.

6 tablespoons
   unsalted butter, softened
1 cup (4 ounces)
   finely grated pecorino or your favorite hard cheese
$3/4$ cup
   all-purpose flour
1 tablespoon, or more
   hot or sweet paprika

white cheddar—bacon
CRACKERS

In a medium bowl, with an electric mixer on low speed or a wooden spoon, beat the butter until light in color, about 1 minute. Add the Cheddar and bacon. Gradually mix in the flour until just combined.

On a sheet of waxed paper, knead the dough a few times. Divide the dough in half. Roll each portion into a 6-inch-long log. Wrap the logs in waxed paper and twist the ends closed. Refrigerate until firm, at least 1 hour or overnight.

Preheat the oven to 350 degrees F. Unwrap the shortbread logs and cut into 1/4-inch-thick slices. Place the slices 1 inch apart on an ungreased or parchment-lined baking sheet. Bake in the center of the oven for about 12 to 15 minutes, or golden. Let the crackers cool on the baking sheet for about 2 minutes, then carefully transfer them to a wire rack to cool completely.

makes about 48 crackers

TIP: Crisply cooked diced pancetta is a wonderful alternative to bacon.

White Cheddar, a fine-quality sharp cheese, is so good with crisp bits of bacon. These will disappear quickly.

$^1/_2$ cup (1 stick)
unsalted butter, softened

1 cup (4 ounces)
grated sharp white Cheddar

2 strips
crumbled bacon, cooked crisp + drained

1 cup
all-purpose flour

In a medium bowl, with an electric mixer on low speed or a wooden spoon, beat the butter and garlic puree until blended. Add the cheese, salt, and cayenne. Gradually mix in the flour until just combined. On a sheet of waxed paper, knead the dough briefly to gather in the loose crumbs. Roll into a 9-inch-long log. Wrap the log in waxed paper and twist the ends closed. Refrigerate until firm, at least 1 hour or overnight.

Preheat the oven to 350 degrees F. Unwrap the log and slice it into $1/4$-inch-thick slices. Place the slices 1 inch apart on an ungreased or parchment-lined baking sheet. Bake in the center of the oven for about 12 to 15 minutes or until very lightly browned at the edges. Let the thins cool on the baking sheet for about 2 minutes, then carefully transfer to a wire rack to cool completely.

makes about 36 thins

ROASTED GARLIC PUREE: Here are 2 ways to roast garlic: Cut the top $1/2$ inch off a whole bulb, drizzle with olive oil, wrap loosely in aluminum foil, roast in an oven at 350 degrees F for 1 hour or until very tender, and then squeeze the whole bulb—the garlic will come out ready to use. Or, cook the peeled cloves from 1 bulb in olive oil to cover about 15 to 20 minutes over medium heat, or until very tender; drain (use the flavored oil for other cooking) and mash with a fork.

makes about $1/4$ cup

TIP: Grated Parmesan or dry Monterey Jack cheese may be substituted for the Asiago.

Roasted garlic and Asiago cheese are the keys to this fragrant shortbread. When raw garlic is roasted, its pungent flavor mellows, making it a great ingredient to use in savory dishes.

$1/2$ cup (1 stick)
unsalted butter
$1/3$ cup
(about $2 1/2$ ounces)
**finely grated
asiago cheese**
$1/2$ teaspoon
salt
pinch
cayenne pepper
$1 1/4$ cups
all-purpose flour

Roasted Garlic
Puree
(recipe follows)

black mustard seed

In a medium bowl, with an electric mixer on low speed or a wooden spoon, beat the butter until light in color, about 1 minute. Add the salt, cheese, and mustard seeds. Gradually mix in the flour until just combined.

On a sheet of waxed paper, knead the dough a few times to gather in loose crumbs. Divide the dough in half and roll each portion into a 6-inch-long log. Wrap the logs in waxed paper and twist the ends closed. Refrigerate until firm, at least 1 hour or overnight.

Preheat the oven to 350 degrees F. Unwrap the shortbread logs and cut into ¼-inch-thick slices. Place the slices 1 inch apart on an ungreased or parchment-lined baking sheet.

Bake in the center of the oven for about 12 to 15 minutes, or until golden at the edges. Let the crisps cool on the baking sheet for about 2 minutes, then carefully transfer them to a wire rack to cool completely.

makes about 48 crisps

Black mustard seeds, used in Indian cooking, are more pungent than the white mustard seeds used in most American mustards. Look for them in Indian markets. They add visual interest and tang to these simple crisps.

7 tablespoons
   unsalted butter, softened
½ teaspoon
   salt
½ cup
(about 2 ounces)
   shredded Monterey Jack cheese
2 teaspoons
   black mustard seeds
1 cup
   all-purpose flour

In a medium bowl, with an electric mixer on low speed or a wooden spoon, beat the butter until light in color, about 1 minute. Beat in the cream cheese, salt, and optional garlic powder until smooth. Scrape down the sides of the bowl with a rubber spatula. Gradually mix in the flour just until combined. Turn the dough out onto a counter and knead a few times until smooth.

Preheat the oven to 350 degrees F. Pinch the dough into scant 1-inch pieces and roll them into balls. On separate squares of waxed paper, scatter each seasoning being used. Roll each ball in one seasoning to coat lightly and place the balls 1 inch apart on an ungreased or parchment-lined baking sheet.

Bake for about 15 minutes, or until just beginning to color. Let the shortbread cool on the baking sheet for about 2 minutes, then carefully transfer to a wire rack to cool completely.

makes about 24 bites

TIP: The stronger the seasoning, the lighter the coating should be. A generous coating of Parmesan is good, but too much cayenne or cracked pepper would be overwhelming. Scattering the flavoring on a flat surface helps to control the amount picked up.

Bites of shortbread, with a hint of goat cheese and garlic, are lightly coated with a variety of seasonings to interplay colors, textures, and flavors.

These take time to do, so I serve them on special occasions with a good Chardonnay or Pinot Noir.

7 tablespoons
  unsalted butter, softened
1 ounce
  goat cheese or cream cheese, softened
$^1/_2$ teaspoon
  salt
$^1/_4$ teaspoon
  garlic powder, optional
1 cup
  all-purpose flour

assorted seasonings
freshly cracked pepper, sunflower seeds, finely grated Parmesan cheese, grated lemon and lime zest, minced fresh herbs, chopped nuts, mustard seeds, paprika with a pinch of cayenne, curry powder, celery seed, dill seed, chili powder, Cajun spices, sesame seeds

Index

Table of Equivalents

the exact equivalents in the following
tables have been rounded for convenience.

abbreviations

US	METRIC
oz=ounce	**g**=gram
lb=pound	**kg**=kilogram
in=inch	**mm**=millimeter
ft=foot	**cm**=centimeter
tbl=tablespoon	**ml**=milliliter
fl oz=fluid ounce	**l**=liter
qt=quart	

weights

US/UK	METRIC
1 oz	30 g
2 oz	60 g
3 oz	90 g
4 oz ($^1/_4$ lb)	125 g
5 oz ($^1/_3$ lb)	155 g
6 oz	185 g
7 oz	220 g
8 oz ($^1/_2$ lb)	250 g
10 oz	315 g
12 oz ($^3/_4$ lb)	375 g
14 oz	440 g
16 oz (1 lb)	500 g
1$^1/_2$ lb	750 g
2 lb	1 kg
3 lb	1.5 kg

oven temperatures

FAHRENHEIT	CELSIUS	GAS
250	120	$^1/_2$
275	140	1
300	150	2
325	160	3
350	180	4
375	190	5
400	200	6
425	220	7
450	230	8
475	240	9
500	260	10

liquids

US	METRIC	UK
2 tbl	30 ml	1 fl oz
$^1/_4$ cup	60 ml	2 fl oz
$^1/_3$ cup	80 ml	3 fl oz
$^1/_2$ cup	125 ml	4 fl oz
$^2/_3$ cup	160 ml	5 fl oz
$^3/_4$ cup	180 ml	6 fl oz
1 cup	250 ml	8 fl oz
$1^1/_2$ cups	375 ml	12 fl oz
2 cups	500 ml	16 fl oz

length measures

$^1/_8$ in	3 mm	6 in	15 cm
$^1/_4$ in	6 mm	7 in	18 cm
$^1/_2$ in	12 mm	8 in	20 cm
1 in	2.5 cm	9 in	23 cm
2 in	5 cm	10 in	25 cm
3 in	7.5 cm	11 in	28 cm
4 in	10 cm	12 in (1 ft)	30 cm
5 in	13 cm